It's All About Gravy

Not All Sauces Are Gravy Recipe Book

by Chloe Tucker

© 2021 Chloe Tucker All Rights Reserved.

License Notes

All rights reserved. This publication cannot be distributed, reproduced, recorded, photocopied, or transmitted. If you desire to share this content, you must seek prior permission from the author. Beware, the author will not be held responsible for your interpretation of this content. However, it is fair to say that the content written herein is accurate.

Table of Contents

Introduction 5

Simple Turkey Gravy 6

Make-Ahead Marsala Turkey Gravy 8

Turkey Mushroom Gravy 11

Special Turkey Gravy 13

Sausage Gravy 15

The Best Turkey Gravy 17

Homemade Chicken Gravy 19

Davy's Gravy 21

Italian Gravy 24

Bill's Sausage Gravy 27

Chef John's Mushroom Gravy 29

Turkey Gravy from McCormick 31

Dad's Hamburger Gravy 33

How to Make Country Gravy 35

Vegetarian Gravy 37

Sausage Gravy 39

Mushroom Cream Gravy Sauce 41

Make-Ahead Turkey Gravy 43

Rich Make-Ahead Turkey Gravy 45

Roast Chicken Pan Gravy 48

Gluten-Free Sausage Gravy 50

Sausage Gravy I 52

Country Sausage Gravy 54

Easy Turkey Gravy 57

Mom's Country Gravy 59

Country Sausage Gravy 61

Savory Turkey Gravy 64

Red Eye Gravy with Ham 66

Southern Style Tomato Gravy 68

Biography 70

An Author's Afterthought 71

Introduction

Just like Bacon, gravy makes everything taste better. There are different types of gravies, depending on where you are located in the United States. From sausage gravy to tomato gravy, redeye gravy, or even chocolate gravy, gravies are spoon-licking good. Whether you know how to make one or not, this recipe book has 30 delicious gravies recipes designed to enhance your meals every time. Anything can be eaten with gravy, and the most popular is biscuit and gravy or thanksgiving roast.

Are you ready to taste some of the best gravies ever? Let's start cooking.

ooooooooooooooooooooooooooooooooooooo

Simple Turkey Gravy

It is simple turkey gravy. My whole family loves it. It takes only 25 minutes to prepare.

Cooking Time: 25 minutes

Serving Sizes: 16

Ingredient List:

- 1/2 cup of Fat from turkey drippings
- Ground black pepper as per your taste
- All-purpose flour - 1/2 cup
- Liquid from turkey drippings - 1 cup
- Turkey stock - 2 cups

ooooooooooooooooooooooooooooooooooooo

Procedure:

Put the fat of turkey drippings in the pan and heat for 3 minutes. Add the flour to it until brown (for 5 minutes).

Put the liquid from turkey stock as well as turkey drippings in the flour mixture. Cook until the gravy gets thick (for 10 minutes). Sprinkle with pepper.

Make-Ahead Marsala Turkey Gravy

Once you make it, and will be addicted to it. My whole family loves it.

Cooking Time: 7 hours 30 minutes

Serving Sizes: 12

Ingredient List:

- Vegetable oil - 2 tsp.
- Onion (chopped) - 1
- Carrot (chopped) - 1
- Coldwater - 2 quarts
- Garlic- 2 cloves
- Butter - 1/4 cup
- Flour - 3 tbsp.
- Salt and ground black pepper to taste
- Turkey necks - 3
- Celery (chopped) - 1 stalk
- Marsala wine - 1/3 cup
- Dried porcini mushrooms - 1/4 ounce
- Bay leaf - 1
- Dried porcini mushrooms - 1/4 ounce
- Heavy cream - 2 tbsp.

OOOOOOOOOOOOOOOOOOOOOOOOOOOOOOOOOOOOOO

Procedure:

Put the oil in a Dutch oven and heat it. Put the turkey necks in it and heat until browned (for 7 minutes). Put the onion, carrot, and celery. Cook them until onion gets tender (for 5 minutes).

Add the Marsala wine to the turkey necks. Let it boil until wine is decreased by half (for 4 minutes).

Now, add water, bay leaf, 1/4 ounce of the mushrooms, and garlic. Let them boil. Cover the oven and cook the meat until tender (for 5 hours). Sieve the turkey stock and allow it to cool (for 2 hours).

Take a mixing bowl and put 1/4 ounce of the porcini mushrooms in it. Pour warm water to cover them. Put a lid on the bowl and put it aside until they get tender (for 15 minutes). Sieve them.

Heat the butter in a pan. Put the diced porcini mushrooms and heat until brown (for 5 minutes).

Add the flour to the butter and mushrooms and cook for 3 minutes.

Put the turkey stock and let it boil. Heat until it gets thickened (for 20 minutes). Now, add cream, pepper, and salt and mix well.

Turkey Mushroom Gravy

I love turkey mushroom gravy. It is very delicious.

Cooking Time: 2 hours 30 minutes

Serving Sizes: 20

Ingredient List:

- Unsalted butter - 2 cups
- Whole white mushrooms - 2 pounds
- Chicken broth - 4 (14.5 ounces) cans
- Chopped onions - 2 cups
- Salt and pepper to taste
- Portobello mushrooms - 1 pound
- All-purpose flour - 1 cup
- Turkey pan drippings - 1 1/2 cups
- Chopped celery - 1 cup
- Cayenne pepper - 1/4 tsp.

ooooooooooooooooooooooooooooooooooooo

Procedure:

Heat the butter in a pot and stir in mushrooms until brown (for 1.30 hours). Take out the mushrooms. Chop them. Put flour in the butter and cook until the mixture gets browned (for 20 minutes). Add the chicken broth and boil it so that it gets thick.

Now, put the drippings in a pan and cook. Put the celery as well as onions and cook until onions get golden (for 20 minutes). Let the gravy boil and then decrease the heat. Cook for 20 minutes. Put chopped mushrooms, cayenne pepper, salt, and black pepper.

Special Turkey Gravy

I love this Turkey gravy. My whole family loves it.

Cooking Time: 30 minutes

Serving Sizes: 20

Ingredient List:

- Turkey drippings - 1 cup
- Turkey stock - 4 cups
- Salt and ground black pepper to taste
- All-purpose flour - 1/4 cup
- Water (optional) - 1/2 cup
- Celery salt - 1 tsp.

ooooooooooooooooooooooooooooooooooooooo

Procedure:

Take a pan and put turkey drippings in the pan. Pour the flour into it. Let it boil and heat until it gets brown (for 5 minutes).

Keep stirring the stock until it gets smooth. Add water if needed.

Stir in the salt, celery salt, and black pepper. Cook the sauce until thickened (for 15 minutes).

Sausage Gravy

Cooking Time: 30 minutes

Serving Sizes: 12

Ingredient List:

- Ground pork sausage - 1 pound
- Milk - 3 cups
- All-purpose flour - 3 tbsp.

oooooooooooooooooooooooooooooooooooooo

Procedure:

Put the sausage in a pan. Cook it until it gets browned. Take the sausage out of the pan and sieve it well. Put it aside.

Discard the fat from the pan except for 3 tbsp.. Again, put the pan to medium heat. Stir in the flour. Stir constantly. Cook for 5 minutes.

Now, pour the milk and mix well. Let it boil until the gravy gets thick.

The Best Turkey Gravy

It is a terrific dish. Once you make it, you will be addicted to it.

Cooking Time: 3 hours 35 minutes

Serving Sizes: 20

Ingredient List:

- Giblets and neck from turkey - 1 1/4 pounds
- Chopped celery - 1 cup
- Dry turkey gravy mix - 2 (1.2 ounces) packages
- Turkey drippings - 1 3/4 cups
- Milk (optional) - 1/2 cup
- Chopped onion - 1 cup
- Ground white pepper - 1 pinch
- Chicken broth - 3 (14.5 ounces) cans
- Quick-mixing flour - 1/4 cup

ooooooooooooooooooooooooooooooooooooo

Procedure:

Put turkey as well as giblets in a pan. Stir in the onion, turkey gravy mix, white pepper, and celery. Put the chicken broth on it and cook it (for 30 minutes). Take out the liver of the turkey and put it aside. Cook it for 2.30 hours. Take out giblets and chop them. Chop the liver as well. Sieve this stock into a pan. Remove bones as well as vegetables.

When the turkey has been roasted, discard the fat from the drippings. Take a mixing bowl and add flour and pan drippings until soft. Add the flour mixture to the stock. Boil the gravy. Put the chopped giblets and chopped liver into it.

Homemade Chicken Gravy

This gravy takes only 30 minutes to prepare and turns out to be super yummy.

Cooking Time: 30 minutes

Serving Sizes: 8

Ingredient List:

- Unsalted butter - 1/2 cup
- Cold chicken stock - 1 quart
- Salt and ground white pepper to taste
- All-purpose flour - 1/2 cup
- Heavy cream - 1/3 cup
- Cayenne pepper - 1 pinch

OOOOOOOOOOOOOOOOOOOOOOOOOOOOOOOOOOOOOO

Procedure:

Heat the butter in a pan to melt. Now, put the flour in the pan and cook for 10 minutes.

Stir in the cold stock. Decrease the heat. Boil it and cook until thickened for 15 minutes. Add the salt, white pepper, cayenne pepper, and heavy cream.

Davy's Gravy

I love this gravy.

Cooking Time: 30 minutes

Serving Sizes: 4

Ingredient List:

- Ground beef - 1 pound
- Cream of mushroom soup - 1 (10.75 ounces) can
- Canned mushrooms - 1 (8 ounces) can
- Steak sauce - 2 tbsp.
- Cider vinegar - 1 tbsp.
- White sugar - 1 tbsp.
- Garlic powder - 1/2 tsp.
- Dried oregano - 1 pinch
- Cornstarch - 1 tsp.
- Onion (chopped) - 1
- Cream of celery soup - 1 (10.75 ounces) can
- Soy sauce - 1 tbsp.
- Worcestershire sauce - 1 tbsp.
- Lemon juice - 1 tbsp.
- Curry powder - 1/2 tsp.
- Cayenne pepper - 1 pinch
- Salt to taste
- Water - 1 cup

OOOOOOOOOOOOOOOOOOOOOOOOOOOOOOOOOOOO

Procedure:

Take a pan and stir in onion as well as ground beef. Fry them until the onion gets tender and the meat becomes brown (for 10 minutes).

Place a pot on the stove over high heat and add the salt, soups, oregano, mushrooms, cayenne pepper, soy sauce, garlic powder, steak sauce, curry powder, Worcestershire sauce, sugar, vinegar, and lemon juice.

Let them boil. Put the meat mixture in it.

Take a mixing bowl and put water as well as cornstarch. Stir until cornstarch gets mixed.

Italian Gravy

Cooking Time: 5 hours 45 minutes

Serving Sizes: 12

Ingredient List:

- Extra virgin olive oil - 2 tbsp.
- Garlic (minced) - 1 clove
- White wine - 1/2 cup
- Dried oregano - 2 tsp.
- Dried thyme - 1 tsp.
- Garlic powder - 3 tbsp.
- Black pepper - 1 tsp.
- Water - 6 cups
- Large yellow onion (diced) - 1
- Pork shoulder roast - 4 pounds
- Water - 3 cups
- Dried parsley - 2 tsp.
- Dried rosemary - 1 tsp.
- Salt - 1 tsp.
- Tomato puree - 2 (28 ounces) cans
- White sugar - 1/4 cup

OOOOOOOOOOOOOOOOOOOOOOOOOOOOOOOOOOO

Procedure:

Put the olive oil in a pot. Fry garlic as well as onions until they become golden. Put the pork shoulder in it and mix well. Add 3 cups of water and 1/2 cup of white wine. Add the oregano, pepper, parsley, salt, thyme, garlic powder, and rosemary. Put the 1/4 spice mixture on the pork. Put a lid on the pot and heat for 30 minutes.

Now, add tomato puree to the gravy. Pour 6 cups of the water into the gravy. Add the sugar as well as the remaining spice mixture to the pot. Cook for 5 hours.

Bill's Sausage Gravy

This creamy sausage gravy is on the list of my often makes. It has simple ingredients, and that's what makes it my favorite.

Cooking Time: 30 minutes

Serving Sizes: 6

Ingredient List:

- Maple-flavored sausage - 1 (12 ounces) package
- All-purpose flour - 1/4 cup
- Salt and pepper to taste
- Butter - 3 tbsp.
- Whole milk - 3 cups

ooooooooooooooooooooooooooooooooooooo

Procedure:

Put the sausage in a pan. Cook it until it gets browned. Take the sausage out from the pan without drippings. Heat butter until it melts. Now, stir in the flour and cook until it gets brown.

Add the milk to the mixture and heat until it gets thick. Sprinkle pepper as well as salt and mix well. Heat for 15 more minutes.

Chef John's Mushroom Gravy

It is so scrumptious. It is very addictive. Children like it the most.

Cooking Time: 1 hour

Serving Sizes: 6

Ingredient List:

- Butter - 1/4 cup
- Salt to taste
- Beef stock - 1 quart
- Thyme leaves (optional)
- Sliced mushrooms - 1 (16 ounces) package
- All-purpose flour - 1/4 cup
- Ground black pepper - 1 pinch

ooooooooooooooooooooooooooooooooooo

Procedure:

Melt the butter in a frying pan. Add the mushrooms to melted butter. Sprinkle the salt and mix well. Cook it for 20 minutes.

Put the flour in the frying pan and cook it for 5 minutes. Now, stir in beef stock and mix all together. Pour the thyme as well as black pepper. Decrease the heat and cook it until the gravy gets thick for 30 minutes.

Turkey Gravy from McCormick

Cooking Time: 5 minutes

Serving Sizes: 4

Ingredient List:

- Gluten-free Turkey gravy nix - 1 (.88 ounce) package
- Water - 1 cup

ooooooooooooooooooooooooooooooooooooooo

Procedure:

Add the water to Gravy Mix in a pan.

Stir frequently. Let it boil. Decrease the heat and cook (for 4 minutes).

Dad's Hamburger Gravy

This is just awesome. I love this hamburger gravy. It is so creamy and thick.

Cooking Time: 30 minutes

Serving Sizes: 6

Ingredient List:

- Lean ground beef - 2 pounds
- Milk - 5 cups
- Butter - 2 tbsp.
- Salt and pepper to taste
- Onion (chopped) - 1/2
- Chicken bouillon granules - 2 tbsp.
- Ground sage - 1 tsp.
- All-purpose flour - 1/2 cup

OOOOOOOOOOOOOOOOOOOOOOOOOOOOOOOOOOOOOOO

Procedure:

Put the beef in a pan. Heat it until it gets brown. Sieve the grease but leave it to coat the surface of the pan. Stir in the onions and heat them until tender.

Now, add 4 cups of milk to the pan. Put the pepper, bouillon, salt, sage, and butter. Boil these for 5 minutes.

Add the flour to a cup of milk and put it in the pan. Cook until the gravy is thickened.

How to Make Country Gravy

I love this creamy gravy. You can enjoy it with anything you like.

Cooking Time: 50 minutes

Serving Sizes: 4

Ingredient List:

- Butter - 2 tbsp.
- Bacon (sliced crosswise) - 4 strips
- All-purpose flour - 1/3 cup
- Salt and ground black pepper to taste
- Chopped green onion - 1 tbsp.
- Breakfast sausage links - 8 ounces
- Chopped green onions - 1/2 cup
- Cayenne pepper - 1 pinch
- Cold milk - 2 1/2 cups
- Cayenne pepper - 1 pinch

OOOOOOOOOOOOOOOOOOOOOOOOOOOOOOOOOOOOOOO

Procedure:

Heat the butter in a pan to melt. Stir in bacon as well as sausage. Stir constantly to make small pieces of the sausage. Cook until bacon becomes crispy and sausage gets brown (for 10 minutes). Now, add 1/2 cup of the green onion to the pan and fry until onions get tender (for 3 minutes).

Put the flour in the mixture until the mixture gets pasty.

Add the milk to the mixture and mix until fully incorporated. Cook until the gravy gets thick (for 5 minutes). Boil the gravy. Sprinkle cayenne pepper, black pepper, and salt. Decrease the heat to low.

Cook the gravy over low heat until thickened for 15 minutes. For garnishing, pour cayenne pepper as well as a green onion.

Vegetarian Gravy

This is great. I love this option for vegetarians.

Cooking Time: 30 minutes

Serving Sizes: 10

Ingredient List:

- Vegetable oil - 1/2 cup
- Garlic (minced) - 5 cloves
- Nutritional yeast - 4 tsp.
- Vegetable broth - 2 cups
- Salt - 1/2 tsp.
- Chopped onion - 1/3 cup
- All-purpose flour - 1/2 cup
- Light soy sauce - 4 tbsp.
- Dried sage - 1/2 tsp.
- Ground black pepper - 1/4 tsp.

OOOOOOOOOOOOOOOOOOOOOOOOOOOOOOOOOOOOOO

Procedure:

Heat a greased pan. Stir in the garlic and onion and fry them until they get tender (for 5 minutes). Now, put the flour, soy sauce, and yeast. Mix all together.

Now pour the broth into the mixture. Sprinkle the sage, pepper, and salt over the mixture and mix well.

Let the mixture boil. Cook the gravy until it gets thick (for 10 minutes).

Sausage Gravy

This gravy is so yummy that you will become addicted. It takes only 25 minutes to prepare.

Cooking Time: 25 minutes

Serving Sizes: 8

Ingredient List:

- Pork sausage - 1 lb.
- Milk - 1 quart
- Buttermilk biscuits
- Flour - 1/3 cup
- Pepper - 1 dash

OOOOOOOOOOOOOOOOOOOOOOOOOOOOOOOOOOOOOOO

Procedure:

Heat the sausage in a pan.

Sieve the fat.

Put the flour on the sausage and mix all together well.

Heat the sausage for 5 minutes.

Pour the milk into the sausage.

Heat until it gets thick.

Sprinkle the pepper and serve the gravy over the biscuits.

Mushroom Cream Gravy Sauce

I make it for special occasions. It is so easy to prepare. You can enjoy it with anything you like.

Cooking Time: 30 minutes

Serving Sizes: 6

Ingredient List:

- Butter - 3 tbsp.
- Garlic (minced) - 2 cloves
- Minced rosemary - 1 tbsp.
- Heavy cream - 1 cup
- Black pepper to taste
- Shallots (minced) - 2
- Sliced button mushrooms - 1 (4 ounces) package
- White wine (divided) - 6 tbsp.
- Sea salt to taste
- Parmesan cheese - 1 tsp.

oooooooooooooooooooooooooooooooooooooo

Procedure:

Melt the butter in a pan. Add the garlic as well as shallots to the pan and cook them (for 3 minutes). Now, put the rosemary as well as mushrooms and mix them well (for 1 minute).

Add the 1/4 cup of white wine to the pan and heat until mushrooms get browned (for 5 minutes). Pour 2 tbsp. of the white wine and cream into the pan. Heat the mixture until the gravy gets thickened (for 5 minutes). Sprinkle the pepper, Parmesan cheese, and salt over the gravy.

Make-Ahead Turkey Gravy

This Turkey gravy is wonderful. I make it for special occasions.

Cooking Time: 2 hours 30 minutes

Serving Sizes: 32

Ingredient List:

- Wings - 6 turkey
- Water - 1 cup
- Chopped carrot - 3/4 cup
- All-purpose flour - 3/4 cup
- Ground black pepper - 1/4 tsp.
- Medium onions - 2
- Chicken broth (divided) - 2 quarts
- Dried thyme - 1/2 tsp.
- Butter - 2 tbsp.

ooooooooooooooooooooooooooooooooooooooo

Procedure:

Heat oven to 400°F. Take a roasting pan and put the turkey wings in it in a layer. Pour the onions on the wings. Place the pan in the oven until the wings become brown (for 1.15 hours).

Put the onions as well as brown wings in a pot. Put in the water, 6 cups of broth, thyme, and carrot in the pot. Let them boil. Decrease the heat and cook for 1.30 hours.

Put the browned wings on a cutting board and remove their skin as well as meat. Sieve the contents of the pot in a pan. Squeeze the liquid from the vegetables. Let the contents boil in the pot.

Take a mixing bowl and combine the flour and 2 cups of chicken broth. Pour it in the boiling turkey broth and cook until the gravy gets thick (for 5 minutes). Add the pepper as well as butter.

Rich Make-Ahead Turkey Gravy

This is super yummy and tasty. I make it on special occasions like Christmas party.

Cooking Time: 3 hours

Serving Sizes: 18

Ingredient List:

- Turkey wings - 3 pounds
- Celery (cut each into 4 equal pieces) - 2 stalks
- Garlic (halved) - 2 cloves
- Chicken broth - 4 cups
- Dried thyme - 1/4 tsp.
- All-purpose flour - 1/2 cup
- Small onions (quartered) - 2
- Carrots (cut each into 4 equal pieces) - 2
- Dry white wine - 1 1/2 cups
- Water - 4 cups
- Butter (optional) - 2 tbsp.
- Salt and ground black pepper to taste

OOOOOOOOOOOOOOOOOOOOOOOOOOOOOOOOOOOOOOO

Procedure:

Heat the oven to 400°F.

Take a roasting pan and put turkey wings, garlic, onions, carrots, and celery. Roast them until wings get browned (for 1 hour and 15 minutes). Now, put these vegetables as well as wings in a pot. Put the pan on 2 stove burners and add white wine to the pan. Cook until there remains only 1/2 cup. Put the mixture in the pan.

Add the water as well as a chicken broth to the pot. Put the thyme and mix it all. Let it boil for 45 minutes. Sieve it and separate meat from cooked wings. Skim the fat and put it in a pan. Now, stir in the butter.

Heat the flour in the fat until browned. Add the broth until the gravy gets thick. Pour the pepper and salt into the gravy.

Roast Chicken Pan Gravy

It is a savory gravy. You would love it. You must give it a try. It takes only 15 minutes to be ready.

Cooking Time: 15 minutes

Serving Sizes: 4

Ingredient List:

- Drippings from a roasted chicken - 1/4 cup
- Cold chicken stock - 2 cups
- All-purpose flour - 2 1/2 tbsp.
- Salt and ground black pepper to taste

OOOOOOOOOOOOOOOOOOOOOOOOOOOOOOOOOOOOOOO

Procedure:

Take a bowl and put the fat of drippings in it. Reserve the fat. Put the flour in the remaining drippings in the pot. Pour 2 tbsp. of the reserved fat into the pot.

Put the pot on the stove and fry the flour until it gets golden (for 5 minutes).

Pour 1/3 cup of the cold chicken stock into the pot. Mix all together. Boil it. Cook it until the gravy gets thickened (for 10 minutes).

Gluten-Free Sausage Gravy

This is a yummy creamy gravy. It is so easy and quick to prepare.

Cooking Time: 35 minutes

Serving Sizes: 16

Ingredient List:

- Bulk pork sausage - 1 pound
- Gluten-free all-purpose baking flour - 10 tbsp.
- Black pepper (divided) - 60 grinds
- Salt to taste (optional)
- Unsalted butter - 1 cup
- Salt - 1 tsp.
- Milk (divided) - 6 cups

ooooooooooooooooooooooooooooooooooooo

Procedure:

Heat a pan. Add sausage to the pan and cook until brown (for 5 minutes). Sieve and remove grease. Decrease the heat to low.

Put the butter in the sausage to melt and add flour—Cook for 10 minutes. Sprinkle 1 tsp. of salt and thirty black peppers.

Increase the heat and add the milk. Let it boil. Cook until the gravy gets thick (for 10 minutes).

Sausage Gravy I

It is superb. It takes only 30 minutes to get ready. It is super yummy.

Cooking Time: 30 minutes

Serving Sizes: 8

Ingredient List:

- Ground pork sausage - 1 pound
- All-purpose flour - 1/4 cup
- Salt - 1/2 tsp.
- Bacon grease - 3 tbsp.
- Milk - 3 cups
- Ground black pepper - 1/4 tsp.

OOOOOOOOOOOOOOOOOOOOOOOOOOOOOOOOOOOOOO

Procedure:

Heat brown sausage in a pan. Put it aside.

Put the bacon grease in the sausage. Stir in the flour and mix well. Keep stirring constantly. Cook the mixture until it gets lightly brown.

Now, add the milk to the pan. Cook the mixture until it gets smooth and thick. Pour the pepper as well as salt into the gravy. Cook it on low heat for 15 minutes.

Country Sausage Gravy

This is my favorite gravy. It is so creamy. You can enjoy it with cookies or anything you like.

Cooking Time: 35 minutes

Serving Sizes: 4

Ingredient List:

- Pork sausage - 1 pound
- Green bell pepper (chopped) - 1
- Garlic (minced) - 2 tbsp.
- Salt and pepper to taste
- Minced sage - 1 tsp.
- Milk (divided) - 2 cups
- Minced parsley - 1/4 cup
- Onion (chopped) - 1
- Crushed red pepper flakes - 1 tsp.
- Unsalted butter - 4 tbsp.
- All-purpose flour - 4 tbsp.
- Minced thyme - 1 tsp.
- Chicken bouillon - 2 cubes

ooooooooooooooooooooooooooooooooooooooo

Procedure:

Heat a pan and stir in the pork, garlic, onion, red pepper flakes, and green pepper. Mix them well and cook until the pork gets granular. Sieve the extra fat except for some amount.

Put the butter, pepper, and salt in the mixture. Mix well and cook until the butter gets melted. Now pour the flour into the mixture and cook it (for 5 minutes). Now, put the thyme as well as sage.

It's time to add milk to the mixture and mix it all together. When the mixture thickens, add more milk. Put the chicken bouillon and heat for 5 minutes.

Put the parsley and 1/4 cup milk just before serving. The gravy will be thick when it cools down.

Easy Turkey Gravy

This is a thick gravy that you can eat with anything. I love it. It would be best if you gave it a try.

Cooking Time: 17 minutes

Serving Sizes: 28

Ingredient List:

- Turkey stock with pan drippings - 5 cups
- Poultry seasoning - 1 tsp.
- Seasoned salt - 1 tsp.
- Milk - 1 cup
- Condensed cream of chicken soup - 1 (10.75 ounces) can
- Black pepper - 1/2 tsp.
- Garlic powder - 1/4 tsp.
- All-purpose flour - 1/3 cup

oooooooooooooooooooooooooooooooooooooo

Procedure:

Boil turkey stock in a pan. Add the soup, poultry seasoning, garlic powder, seasoned salt, and pepper. Cook it on low heat.

Put milk in the oven and let it warm. Add flour to it and put this mixture in the gravy. Cook the gravy until it thickens (for 1 minute).

Mom's Country Gravy

This is quick and easy to make. It takes only 20 minutes to get ready.

Cooking Time: 20 minutes

Serving Sizes: 6

Ingredient List:

- Vegetable oil - 1/2 cup
- Salt - 1 tsp.
- Milk - 4 cups
- All-purpose flour - 3/4 cup
- Ground black pepper - 1 tsp.

OOOOOOOOOOOOOOOOOOOOOOOOOOOOOOOOOOOOOOO

Procedure:

Heat a greased frying pan. Put flour, pepper, and salt in the hot oil until it gets smooth. Heat it until it gets brown (for 10 minutes).

Keep stirring it to avoid lumps. Cook it until it becomes thick. Enjoy it with your family.

Country Sausage Gravy

This is creamy and delicious.

Cooking Time: 35 minutes

Serving Sizes: 4

Ingredient List:

- Pork sausage - 1 pound
- Green bell pepper (chopped) - 1
- Garlic (minced) - 2 tbsp.
- Salt and pepper to taste
- Minced sage - 1 tsp.
- Milk - 2 cups
- Minced parsley - 1/4 cup
- Onion (chopped) - 1
- Red pepper flakes - 1 tsp.
- Unsalted butter - 4 tbsp.
- All-purpose flour - 4 tbsp.
- Minced thyme - 1 tsp.
- Chicken bouillon - 2 cubes

oooooooooooooooooooooooooooooooooooooo

Procedure:

Heat the pork, garlic, onion, red pepper flakes, and green pepper in a hot frying pan until the pork gets tender. Remove extra fat but not all.

Add the butter, pepper, and salt to the pork mixture. Heat them until the butter gets melted. Gradually, stir in the flour. Mix all together and heat it for 5 minutes. Stir constantly. Now, put the thyme as well as sage.

Add half a cup of milk one by one. Mix all together. The mixture will become thick. Now, stir in more milk. Don't boil it. Put in the chicken bouillon. Heat it for 5 minutes. When the mixture gets thick, pour more milk on it.

Before serving it, pour the 1/4 cup of milk as well as parsley.

Savory Turkey Gravy

It is a spicy gravy.

Cooking Time: 20 minutes

Serving Sizes: 24

Ingredient List:

- Turkey stock - 5 cups
- Water - 1 cup
- Salt - 1 tsp.
- Celery salt - 1/4 tsp.
- All-purpose flour - 1/4 cup
- Poultry seasoning - 1 tsp.
- Ground black pepper - 1/2 tsp.

OOOOOOOOOOOOOOOOOOOOOOOOOOOOOOOOOOOOOOOO

Procedure:

Boil the turkey stock in a skillet over medium heat. Put the flour in water in a mixing bowl and mix them well.

Now, pour the turkey stock into the flour mixture and combine well. Stir in the poultry seasoning, celery salt, pepper, and salt. Let them boil and then decrease the heat. Cook for 10 minutes until the gravy gets thick.

Red Eye Gravy with Ham

This gravy is so enriched. My whole family loves it. It is a quick and easy recipe.

Cooking Time: 30 minutes

Serving Sizes: 4

Ingredient List:

- Vegetable oil - 1 tbsp.
- All-purpose flour - 1 tsp.
- Cayenne pepper - 1/8 tsp.
- Brewed coffee - 2/3 cup
- Chopped fatty ham scraps - 1/2 cup
- Salt and black pepper to taste
- Ham - 4 (1/4 inch thick) slices

oooooooooooooooooooooooooooooooooooooooo

Procedure:

Add oil to the frying pan. Put the ham scraps in the hot frying pan and cook until they get brown (for 5 minutes). Transfer to a bowl and reserve some grease.

Add the ham slices to the frying pan. Heat them until they get brown (for 5 minutes). Sprinkle the salt, cayenne pepper, and black pepper on ham slices. Transfer the ham to a bowl.

Decrease the heat and put the flour in the frying pan drippings. Heat it for 2 about minutes. Now, increase the heat and add the coffee to the frying pan. Whisk constantly. Heat it until it gets thick. Again, put the ham in the frying pan so that it becomes warm.

Southern Style Tomato Gravy

This tomato gravy is super yummy. It takes only 35 minutes to be ready.

Cooking Time: 35 minutes

Serving Sizes: 16

Ingredient List:

- Bacon - 1 (1 pound) package
- Flour - 2 tbsp.
- Salt - 2 tsp.
- Cream cheese (optional) - 1 (3 ounces) package
- Butter - 1 tsp.
- Whole tomatoes - 2 (28 ounces) cans
- Ground black pepper - 4 tsp.
- Heavy cream - 1/2 cup

OOOOOOOOOOOOOOOOOOOOOOOOOOOOOOOOOOOOOOOO

Procedure:

Heat bacon in a pan until it gets brown (for 10 minutes). Reserve drippings in the pan. Sieve the bacon.

Put flour as well as butter in bacon drippings. Cook until it starts to get thick (for 3 minutes). Add tomatoes to it and sprinkle pepper and salt. Pour heavy cream as well as cream cheese. Cook until thick (for 10 minutes).

Biography

For decades, this beautiful actress graced our screens with her incredible talent and performance in movies that captivated the script and emotions of the viewers. Well, life rarely goes as planned, but we should always make the best out of it, like Chloe.

Originally from the bubbly city of Los Angeles, she has moved from the movie industry into the food scene. Her role in Mama Mia ignited her passion for food. She has taken the New York scene by surprise. Charmed by the unique regions she had visited, the delicious delicacies she tasted, her uncanny appreciation for flavors, ingredients, and cooking techniques have continued to wow customers wide and far.

However, as mentioned, she started as an actress. Breaking into the food scene was easy because she had contacts and connections, but satisfying clients was a different ball game. Over the years, she has mastered the food scenes and unique flavors clients seek. Today, her clients can attest to the high-quality food from her restaurants.

The New York food scene is a jungle that only the strong dare to tread. However, she was a passionate student and learned the tricks and tips, and slowly set her passion for delivering excellent tastes to all who sought them.

An Author's Afterthought

Did you like my book? I pondered it severely before releasing this book. Although the response has been overwhelming, it is always pleasing to see, read or hear a new comment. Thank you for reading this and I would love to hear your honest opinion about it. Furthermore, many people are searching for a unique book, and your feedback will help me gather the right books for my reading audience.

Thanks!

Chloe Tucker

Made in the USA
Las Vegas, NV
11 December 2023

82515540R00039